A Hotel in Belgium

# A Hotel in Belgium

Brett Fletcher Lauer

Four Way Books
Tribeca

Please direct all inquiries to:
Editorial Office
Four Way Books
POB 535, Village Station
New York, NY 10014
www.fourwaybooks.com

Library of Congress Cataloging-in-Publication Data

Lauer, Brett Fletcher.
[Poems. Selections]
A hotel in Belgium / Brett Fletcher Lauer.
pages cm
Includes index.
ISBN 978-1-935536-39-0 (alk. paper)
I. Title.
PS3612.A94273H68 2014
811'.6--dc23
2013036090

This book is manufactured in the United States of America and printed on acid-free paper.

Four Way Books is a not-for-profit literary press. We are grateful for the assistance
we receive from individual donors, public arts agencies, and private foundations.

[clmp]

We are a proud member
of the Council of Literary Magazines and Presses.

Distributed by University Press of New England
One Court Street, Lebanon, NH 03766

## Contents

"It is as if a curtain had been drawn from before my soul, and this scene of infinite life had been transformed before my eyes into the abyss of the grave, forever open wide."

—Goethe

for my brothers,
Josh, Deakin, and Judd

# Poem

A pond where one person comes to notice the other,
where the other becomes an answer. The shape
of this construct is a world. The world is made of each

reflected across the lakes and ponds of a region
known for its bodies of water. Each is conditional
without the other, without each other the world

looks sterile. The world is made of roses
and ivory, each rose has petals to be plucked
during a nervous spell, a sudden phrase:

watching a boat drifting off without oars.
Without each other, there is no answer. A mist
of roses surrounds the lovers. There is a house

of ivory on a hill, it will hide their story. Each thinks
this as they enter: There is a shape to the one I love,
potential would not exist without this. Cardinals

in maples could not be filled with song. Without
each other there is no one to answer. Despair sets in,
a mistake, a phrase: the silhouette as she enters.

With the onset of darkness each is filled with
the onset of longing. The lovers set out to discover
each other, almost as ivory, almost as roses near

evening open to themselves. We construct a world.
The world is made of this room. This room made
of chance. The day is ordered for such purpose.

# I

# Majestic Interlude

The rainy season is a league away traveling
at the speed of an era. The cloud formation
does not dissolve as I remove my eyes

from my palms. I can no longer walk the distance.
Insects congeal beneath my skin in order
to rest. I think of a number between one and ten

and a ditch to place my body in, shallow
enough to fill—a single spade of gravel
to cover my mouth and one for each eye.

Like emulsion, I want to remember
what I have touched, the universe
that crushes; the black smoke across

the lips as night crows speak
of floodwaters, the trees falling quietly
at night, and the night quietly falling at sea.

A cold morning keeps me frozen in position.
The heat from the vent near my ribs
is invisible and comforts me.

A filtration device is attached to my lungs.
I have reached the number designated
as the halfway marker. Soon I will possess

no more ideas. I am further along
than I imagined I would be. When my body
is covered, a mound will be formed.

Someone will find me fixed in place.
Rain is falling over the sea and the sea
begins to arrive. The banks of the ditch

slide over my limbs. I am having difficulty
being. Someone will find me. The night crows
are silent. They are perched on my knees.

# Stockholm Syndrome

In the beginning, my eyes were angled
out a window on a point providing
conclusion while periodic vibrations
of fear aggressively governed
my anatomy. There were others
kept ignorant of the latitude of this
municipality, the river's proper name,

and its source in a local mountain.
It's important this isn't construed as
a sales pitch, just a sensible presentation
of the future, sealed as it is in caskets
like some distant city encircled by
horned predators. Don't wish the dead
are not. They are. It's easier to close

your eyes, conclude we earn equal reward,
partial, or none, as there aren't 30 lives
to expend, or we would have reclined
on premium memory foam awaiting
the 29th. In the beginning, day
effortlessly transported an invisible
thread, connecting vagueness to a gray

light fading. Please believe me, it is
in your interest to bend your head
as a diversion from eye contact, small
talk in the off-hours of private enterprise.
I feel I must reiterate there were others,
our eyes all averted out the window
while the sun's procedure diminished

words on book spines—a third of them
 persisted in the shadows like heirlooms
in a vacant room. My head was bent,
 was always bent, a diversion from blame
and consequence—knowing that if
 one rises for any occasion, one
generally finds oneself a good way on

 the mountain path, accompanied by
functionaries, clerks, and stand-ins,
 with their dogmatic attachment to doubt,
faultfinding, or the reveries regarding
 transfers to a more temperate time zone.
I won't account for their pilgrimages,
 plotted, embarked on, or satisfied.

I will only say some ventured outdoors
 and could not return. The vast majority
found relief in voices acting as a proxy
 to stars, to evening's arrival predicted
as a literal tilting away. I should
 remark there were plotlines, instances
of false contentment, and misadventures

 contributing to this particular state,
which found a corollary in late autumn
 foliage placed in a vase on a table
to better contemplate the color
 from the couch. It failed to entertain
or actively dispense with sorrows
 or, worse, the lack thereof. Take today,

ceiling fan and gray tiles—this interior
humming is a scheme justifying
deactivation. At random I lay my
hand on the volume required to fact-check
the forthcoming treatise *Six Million*
*Ways to Die*. It might be easier to say
fortune is a form of alarm-mongering,

that even the clouds composing sunset
beyond the peaks do so with free will,
shaped as nothing a hand could shape.
I'm beginning to lose my interest.
I'm trying to say it with feeling: Every
person I love is here. Those who
elected to leave, can't stay.

# Throughout Winter

The occasion is marked with impurities, with swans
quieted or frozen, with minor crimes committed
near nightfall, with bottles and bottles of wine,

with Possibly until No, until there is no one left
in the mirror. I rise to look in the mirror. Gone
are the days of finding myself, of celebrating victory:

whistles, streamers, and objects that shake down
like blooms. Their absence is troublesome.
The occasion is marked with gardens wild, belling

throughout winter. With a well-kept air I explain
I am a fixed principle, then bury my hands.
Thus I am marked throughout winter. Thus I rise

and stand in line to be marked throughout winter.
Gone the days chiseled from stone. Gone the days
this was a town. Gone those who spoke of fleeing.

Gone sand and hourglass—the lions are pacing
at the gates. I explain my tears shift from one vessel
to another and taste of anise, then bury my hands

until I am unsure my hands are my hands, are such
fixed principles. Gone are the days of wine and glass
to be filled. Gone the chiseled stone like the tattoo

of a name. Thus I change the tattoo of my name into
a lion's profile and bleed for days. The absence
of a name is troublesome. The occasion will be

marked with a long winter, will be fixed and etched in the mirror. The mirror will be hung at the gate.

# A Hotel in Belgium

I collapsed in the railway station, and without
a calling card, I was not curable, so they
positioned me in a house with blue doors
and curtains pulled shut. My inability
for another language kept me bound

to a single room, though the service was
impeccable: small pieces of chocolate
in the shapes of familiar animals. I walked
from the miscellaneous into the astral body.
I was told somewhere there was a royal

staircase and a country of horses grazing
in empty fields, but the horses are terribly sad
without a rider. I stripped away my aristocratic
clothing, my tight-fitting hose, my pointed
leather shoes, my doublet, and sheer tunic.

Finally I discarded my timeless diamonds
and then, and then I went looking for a rider.
I collapsed in the railway station and was given
holy tablets and truth serum. For days I could
not eat, all the cooked goods cooled and needed

breathing on: *Nurse, will you whisper over this*
*lamb leg.* I want my sauces delicious and warm,
carnivorous with spice. I don't want a spoon,
to use a dressing case or study with the bishop.
I despise the mirror, its inability to understand

(I don't have a normal penis). I ring the nurse
twice a day, am told somewhere there is
a teaspoonful of country air that cures any ailment.
The larva grows and swells my limbs, a heavy
winter coat in the fall that sheds with spring.

Every single morning the nurses tell me a strong
horse gets up and moves in small circles around
larger circles. I must be a little horse, inconspicuous
and of little significance. My brightest star is
barely of the sixth magnitude, but it's still a star.

## Staged Darkness

I don't think you understand this is narrated
by a dead man and you won't hear a thing
when you don't understand words in books

or films, acknowledge interference patterns
being dragged from center screen to a new world
not *the* New World. That might be a warning.

Stay guard-like, curious conditions crop up
like a half-brother discovered middle-aged
on a sickbed at the novel's end. We sit close,

watch tomato plants in the garden grow
yellow, a definition of boredom in poems
or a movie unless foreign from each other,

and this unique moment acts as communication
working in opposition to the mistrust flowering
in geometric designs. If we can say we are here,

*here* requires explanation as to the lateness
of the civilian day. That might be a threat.
At a minimum, shut the door. Shut the door,

it's dictated by a script absent myth, foxes
returning with messages to a representative
tree in the observed world or to the bank

of a river appearing on the left of the way
we read. Do you recall that exact act, scene, line?
I stood by morning shores with similar grayness

washing gray skin, under a familiarly staged
sun spotlighting where each drowned: the infirm,
unprovoked children, lovers from time immemorial

before photography replicated perspective
with funeral music. Even in death, I've always
been this dull—but it matters what we name

the characters, each difference between patient
and client, firstborn, husband, neighbor,
their roles and how suffering enters the public

domain. Tell me, sister or wife, have we spoken
like this before, powerless and on the record?
It's time to acknowledge a contrary narrative:

The part of me you touched was barely authentic,
like a custom-made backdrop with painted coral,
the outline of a shipwreck, and gothic sea creatures

posed in their own bad light. To my detriment, I think
I always hated you. Even before you delivered
your famous monologue, your face was ruined.

# Topics for Amplification

The head is seized with a dizziness while reading
devotional literature in this queer light; a fifth-
hand account of a thousand gray stars prearranged
to shine so-so over the wonders of modern cities,
like fables lacking blood spilled judiciously across

a forest floor, and the moral lesson we look for
won't materialize at the business park while gazing
on the pond's moonlit surface. Kindness conjured
will never kill anything enough. All the microscopic
hours spent viewing your face proved abstract,

like the "world" "out there," a landscape observed
with a rarefied air until it splintered off in rain.
In this queer light, no voyage expresses itself literally
anymore, a descriptive sentence regarding riding
Mongolian horses on dusty terrain cues civilization,

which is one way of saying the march of events,
another, the bell tower tolls a directive. You hear the bells?
Of course you hear the bells. Flipping forward
thirty pages in the primer, past three chapters
detailing the new wilderness, symbolic discharges,

sundials chopping day into shadows, the text
specifies ending in departure, death, or slightly
more ambiguous topics to spin off into stories from
a nearer future where guards announce the dawn
and others echo this call until all gates are opened.

A comprehensive discussion is out of place here.
We can't assess the damages with defective instruments.
Stay indoors, the world out there is a chronic sedative,
a time clock set in motion with coins deposited by
a person. Please don't disagree with me, a person

does something "of his own accord" or without self-
control, designs change even conditions we haven't
actually experienced. Wait another day in this queer light,
in this fragmentary present state in lieu of a whole
no longer in vogue, and time keeps on ticking, will

keep on ticking on a watch decreased in resale value.
The hurt continuing to hurt is a descriptive phrase
for how we might view the foot traffic on the street
in this queer light, occupying a head with some shame,
willing to incite harm in summer months or recession.

Allow the passage of time, delay soliloquies, return
to thinking precisely about thinking too precisely.
You feel the way you do, that's fine. Skies clear, azure
patterns are composed, and you continue walking
toward what you knew all along you weren't going to reach.

## *from* A Thorn of Sonnets

The hum has died down, it does sometimes
in town, somewhere in the glimmering world.
However theatrical it sounds, we must start
whether a voice calls petitioning our ease or not.
Green things will continue living in winter.
It happened before, once and then twice,
at a dead hour, friends went away. I'm unable
to articulate their names. A man died.
One spoke twenty-two words: This evening snow
begins its particular melody of the so-called
Swedish nightingale; this evening the windowpane
caught a bird tenderly, without malice. Nowadays
it is a rule, snow scatters where your foot
threads. In any soul there is a bright cross of antlers.

# Falter, Sigh, and Lightly Tremble

Once you have left a boy, you stand
bannerless, hair pushed from face
to shoulders. Most stories bend something

like this: boy breaking heart hunching
off in grayish rain; boy held more by ideas
than sensations, with how the puddle

in the courtyard empties than with
thinking *tremendous how sensitive my nipples*
*are under these sheets*. Once you break

you remake yourself between the sound
of a castanet and the size of a shadow cast.
And you do and you will once you have

left a boy. Though tonight under lambskin
and red light, a blue flame voids
the mouth with each kiss. And tomorrow

one wakes to skies where everything
hangs and hearts section off into irregulars,
and—waking—one is anew, so the story

would have you, until gray swarming
blurs recent events, particulars, how evening
was cast: a subtle shift in degrees as a dream

once wide awake won't resurface or, rather,
as is said, the brightness of day finds
each corner. For tonight, for once pretend

you are a corner rather than find one;
what could happen through this window,
a skyline, and a river reformats itself,

which means things are happening and you
can fake your way through this without being
mocked or mocking, without referring to

a second more dead language, meaning
it is read, but at dinner talked around,
saying perhaps your scarf is aquamarine

with little goldfish, and yes, your elegant
wristwatch just stopped. Temporarily
your mouth fails to perform simple tasks

like radiance or swallow, and your face
requires you imprint the image of a face
across your face, across your face

fingerprints, smudges on lips. Breath
that isn't private touches variously on necks.
It doesn't matter who bends toward you,

how well you dance in the corner, or that
stars broadcast feverishly with prophecies.
You should just keep quiet, you don't

want to be whatever I said you are.

# The Portable Twentieth Century

I stand near an open window, various domestic
ornaments interchangeable, given names withdraw
further. A blue bud vase holds a solitary flower.
I'm unable to summon the variety, the flower
the color of the wallpaper, the wallpaper based
on symmetry adhering to conventions of genre
with a fever. Temperatures change, it rains,
or maybe the timeline was free of precipitation.
Recall the walks around a man-made lake with you,
a hand held out indefinitely in the wind.
Everything was almost real or a type of real
regarded as orthodox, how a text became emblematic
of a section of voice overheard in my head
from farther above, a voice all day speaking.
I made judgments accordingly, rather than review
comprehensive but unavailable data. Choices
appeared best made about a past that didn't happen.
It can be embarrassing when things happen.
There were alternatives. I opened doors and
windows to smell ripening fruit, to justify
chronology as being relatively predictable, even if
an intervention could have been attended differently.
Do not fear dreaming these vivid memories which
might be false. Almost everything sometimes is
placed in a hierarchy: A good year is a year
is a lapse in time. I'm likely to tell difference
based on how things physically felt. How much more
is there? I remember. Eye colors in certain angles
of light. I didn't fear the dreams, incidents transpired
in a manner so boring I fell asleep. For a moment
I was imagining I was you. I remember bystanders
and encoded dialogue. These stay, overlap, fade

into an attention: I stood with an ideal attitude
toward the wind, the flower purely physical,
the vase almost blue. In the absence of perfect
information, this is for your eyes only. In this
perfect absence, absence is like information.

## Model Community

Naturally a tree is cut and the house built becomes
a village, the scenic village becomes a town
missionaries pass through en route to an incorporated

district where prayers find donors to knock on, and
the town manufactures a city observed from a small
hill that spreads to the valleys east and west at least

until shoreline. In the western corner, the heart
has previously gone in and out of fashion and in this
news cycle is experiencing great heights. Residents

old-timey or new continue unmarked with a sign
yet continue to walk with the strut of a person marked
by a sign, publicly touch flowers, determined in that

cruel manner to wait for transformation—the absence
of a clear cause and effect creates an illusion of opportunity
like new luxury condos near industrial docks. As planned,

what rain falls here finds a stream determined for such
purpose, as a ghost might serve the purpose of fortune.
Filled with wonder and California weather, the historic

architecture indicates streets worth walking, makes
waking up and descending upon them a noble pursuit
until the path winds with intention or accident, and here

we are, clearly standing staring down into the full luster
we named Elixir Valley. I'm too bored to look,
get up from the futon, get through this year sending

postcards of cloudless days our imagination required.

## An Index of Wind

THE CITY'S POPULATION OF WIND is dwindling, escaping farther and farther to the outer suburbs, past the last station stop. No one speaks of civilized wind, the bygone days. The wind in the corner is blushing, hair in its eyes, too shy to utter a syllable. A country wind is for flying elaborate kites shaped like triplanes and camouflaged in clouds high above fields bending toward future fields. Only visionaries speak of "crazy wind." Crazy wind touches the sky. Crazy wind is a tender child beneath a madrone tree. Crazy wind drunk on wine. Dark wind in the evening, sailors stop breathing. Diacritical wind alters the world, how we speak it. Doctor wind is saving a woman on an operating table somewhere between here and now. No one speaks of the dwarf wind, a small wisp around the ankles, what shuffles beneath the bottom of a door, all doors. The famous wind is announced with bugles, with banners trimmed with tassels; a motorcade drives the famous wind to make a speech regarding its relationship to Western Wind. The theoretical wind is a grand forecast, while the teleprompting wind is scrolling: There is no child dancing in the wind, no spring wind in London, no wind begging to rock the grass, no garden wind to give life to the man trapped like wind, no solemn wind, no one alone with the solemn prairie wind, no wind that moves like a cripple among the leaves, the wind is without pathos, passively attending, and crossing the brown land.

# For Example

Arrangements were made to secure myself
away from you, in numerous places far
and near, with a near-perfect clock keeping

time as precipitation multiplied across
ten million lakes waiting or snow fell
on Union Street in Brooklyn. During this

entire interlude, a subject was in mind;
each morning, concluding my inventory,
I devoted several hours to its purpose

until a sentence repeated contained no signal.
Then evenings, several shooting stars
were accidentally seen, then apparently

gone, like actors finishing a thought with a stance
or gesture to heighten the drama's subtext.
The exit, though, didn't correspond so much

as the entries you had with others, often
with parts quite obscured. It was, then, as if
a single remark might sometimes refer

to a false geography, sometimes a bridge
leading away from an island and sometimes
the clockworks abandoned on that island.

## *from* A Thorn of Sonnets

Passing years, at their most destructive,
have scope enough to contain transformation
by violence. Repair condition: The glass
means mirror. Hours pass and refer to seasons.
To destroy the lovely body threatens
to destroy the family, the house to which
one belongs, and possibly His image.
Not the wax but the stamp that marks it.
An object declares ambition: not to write
about beauty. It seems less and less
probable that there shall be no death
freed from emotional reference. Scattered
feelings grow. In the later sonnets implications
of this desire are pursued.

# In a Station of the Metro

Our situation is complicated, full of negations
and negations of negations. To remember

experience rather than what's occurring—
this detachment replaced with strangers

other strangers recognize. It will be repeated
in a station of the metro, rain and silence,

revisions of subjectivity propose the rain
manufactures the rain devoid of hymns.

One form of memory is forgetting another.
For instance, I wanted to do something great

for God, a sanctuary against the world
in a faraway city. To condemn those who are

hazardous, particularly regarding suicide.
A lament is knowing that a man's body is found

most often in the room where breathing ceased
beside lines composed for a future phantom.

It was a sufficiently sympathetic room for the sick,
to say little of how mundane the view, how birds

refused candor for branches in the center of a forest
at an hour both poetic and prosaic, an hour when

a book is closed, a letter signed with sudden emotion.
Strange revisions of thought manufactured darker

reflections set down during the composition of this
letter, sent from one hand to another chronology

and held at the frame of evening with its status
of personal utterance repeated, as if to say, as if to say.

# The Collected Poems

I'm sure you're just dying to look
at another poem, in which the head
of the narrator requires clearing
at five-hour intervals—the clicking
wrist a rest, the eyes from caffeine,
panic, excessive crying, and/or
the abundance of mental pictures—
to shut down and reboot. Another
poem which seems to suggest
the possibility that the video
of a rabbit befriending a red fox
somewhere in Montana or Europe
and sent to me sometime after
midnight by a friend in Oakland
could be an accurate metaphor
for an emotional state in simpler
times we might have named "grace"
and turned to Webster's to quote
the definition. Reason stands
that the present unease isn't alleviated
easily enough with toxins and tar.
I watch the video again. It is always
the people I knew and/or liked
the least who update me the most,
and there is no effort to leave
my mid-century chair to set aside
time for a host of novel hobbies
such as gardening, kayaking, or swap
meets meant to develop into a new
lifestyle routine. Nothing transports
me enough, not even the novella I left
on the nightstand at my parents'

summer cottage about a Swiss-German
  child named Sinclair, who is under
duress, not so much as a device
  to embark upon a monologue in which
certain ideas gradually atrophy but so
  we can better judge his later stance
toward family, the institution of marriage,
  and his school days. It is just easier
to conjure an elsewhere, a sickly look
  cultivated over a decade, I've done it
for the job, all manner of morning
  and evening commutes—but no profit-
making patent exists. It's for the best
  I sit this out near the radiator painted silver,
a decoupage plate fashionably nailed
  to the wall, reading another poem, where
the narrator is confused and probably feels
  little or nothing and stands to look
out the window at the starlight stalking
  the river to better contemplate the variety
of thoughts responding to outside factors.
  It's easy to believe the streets are watching—
boulevard shadows shift over the faces
  of strangers propped against the railing
of a bridge on the Eastern Seaboard
  or any number of anonymous arenas
visible from here. It should be easy
  to feel, and I want to feel an affinity
with the Swiss-German child who
  is mistakenly called "princess," until
the sentence arrives when he gives in
  and answers the salutation. I don't care

how it ends. To be honest, when
  the number of sufferers jumps to even
two, statistically my sympathy is depressed.

# No New Information

When I hang in the air
it will be by popular
demand. There is
a contingency of people
who think loving me
is wrong. I made this
for them. I care deeply
about our republic
but I'm unsure what
to do next. I'm lonely.
Duh. Even I can learn
to endure but can
no longer speak
for us. Your anxiety
is noted. There is
something radically wrong
in the letter I left
or else Scandinavian.
I feel my apartment
getting dirty. I make
a cup of tea. It is
an accomplishment.
Later, I'm going
to haunt everything
in this room.

# A Home for Head Injuries

Take me to a warm room and keep me
lying flat. Place a small pillow
beneath my injured head. My eyes

may eventually go blank, always when
most excited. They may begin losing
perspective: The sun is in my throat.

Please loosen the clothing around my neck.
I am beginning to see a dome of light.
It is a shrinking habitat. I might say:

My tongue weighs tons and is made of sulfur.
I might say: My tongue is mostly phosphorus,
my lashes carry salt. Where was I going?

I was heading in a direction. You know
how it must feel to make an admission.
It is easy to forgive. It is asked for. It is given.

Bring me back indoors, undress me, place me
in a bed and sponge my body freely
with seawater until my temperature drops.

I can get upset by the easiest of things:
blood near my eyes. The bleeding point
most likely in the lungs, stomach, or skull.

Until I become fully conscious prop me
on my side to keep airways open.
I am frightened. It is difficult to grieve.

I am thinking it is cold, it is only morning.
I am uneasy on land and water.
My head hurts and I am trying to explain

that each person has a partner on the opposite coast.
When the two partners find each other
they sit down together and wait by the sea.

Everything is calm, peaceful, and cold.
People are arriving to build a home
near the sea. The sea will be late to arrive.

## The Revised Script

In earlier drafts, the sea's
 function was utilitarian.
It was placed for sentimental
 reasons and to set the scene
for the meeting of two
 protagonists—officially
man and woman introduced
 by arrangement of a third
party at an office function
 or, if desirable, chance:
a Jane Austen novel, a seaside
 bench. The lights go down
and occasionally through
 ambivalent darkness
a horn is heard from
 a ship at rest, quarantined
with illness, either mild
 or severe. The lights, after
a prescribed intermission,
 rise. I know the declarations
from the middle scenes
 serve to prove one will let
the other down, and now,
 two-thirds through, a slight
fatigue sets in. What was
 spring fades now into

autumn, and what was
  1986 passes into updated
hairstyles and footwear.
  I understand the linear passage
of time arranges them here,
  and furthermore he or she
may be holding an object
  providing behavioral cues. A book
by Charlotte Brontë. A red
  umbrella. It goes unnoted
in dialogue, that is to say it is
  taken for granted. The lights go down.
The lights come up. Enter clouds.
  Not for anything, but even
pleasure felt well enough
  is a form that plays itself out
with second-guessing. We can
  recall being here before
on a seaside bench where ships
  unload crates or cruise passengers.
It goes unnoted but is clear
  with time foreshortened that he
or she or one of us is here
  to portray the other differently,
aided by stage directions
  and body language—that said

person has changed, grown,
  or moved on. Occasionally
a ship's horn is heard, enters into
  thought to be experienced
as another analogous instance
  of morbid conditions prevailing.
The time remaining moves
  forward with a new slant or is
abandoned in case of rain.
  It can't be undone, it won't be
undone, it is done for the sake
  of drawing this out. A part
was played, and the wind kept
  interrupting his or her face
with hair, obviously a mistake
  we will call the natural elements
that no script anticipated.

# II

# Community of Inquiry

The lying machine looks out over the map.

It looks east. It looks west. Both reoccur
in gloom. Evening lets down its history,

particular and carefree, without a station
to look or love from. This means no story,

no once upon a time near a holy house
in the country did children sing in a field

slowly becoming money. The children
are lying down to sleep, intoxicated

with environment, with a blueness,
a version of its own hue happening above

their heads, looking like a certain place
imagined and shown to our imagination

as different each time, each time flowers
something the opposite of work. Each

thinks essentially *No more tears,* then releases
more tears from no specific external event

but from the privacy that exists
within them. They are fixed on every

minute of the day. The day knows
its inhabitants can't leave or rather can

but won't. An inner disturbance spreads.

# A Romantic Notion

On the first day, this and that, flowers form, organisms originate in panda parts and pattern an entire population problem, the humming in the ears is transposed into distant shadowy objects so that a symbol is thought to be heard in the shifting leaves—a name, a body, a voice reading aloud from an original copy of a text against which, somewhere, diligently a proofreader follows the printed proof. On the second day, a white-noise machine putters, each serpent continues eating each serpent's tail, an acorn converts to oak, and the river is resetting. There is something for everyone, lack of family support or not, a community launches clouds dyed the contemporary hue of wool. On the third day, the town remains conspicuously absent of games of chance, Halloween, or the mention of intimate body parts. I'm busy buying a device pictured on TV that prunes the lawn. Witness its prongs! So sturdy they carry a raccoon carrying a trout over the property line and there you have it, another nuisance gone. Avoid speaking generally about flora and fauna, changing codices of splendor containing music for feasts, or absentee fathers. It should be enough that the trees sway with a romantic notion, shake with inconsequence. On the fourth day, ask me if I care. On the fifth day, from a distance more accurate, we observe antique days from a mountain once a hill, once a voice reciting by the water, waiting for seasons to alter, a fish to fossilize. On the sixth, nothing happens. I'm entering my middle style. I'm being treated well for my depression. I worry tomorrow's forecast is an alternative version of this—that one winter will mean snow and the other rain. On the seventh day, I'm waiting by the mailbox for a device advertised to capture a sunset forever in order to never climb the mountain again for a conversation about "sunsets" as the sun sets at the same time at the same location—5:25 p.m. on Elixir Ridge—and then again once or twice more a thousand miles from here where this hill has become a forest or a sea.

# Seaside Suicide

The scene is segmented and plotted, a landscape
painters devise. The hills are not one-dimensional,
and in their dips the deer lean their blue antlers
toward heather. So general to be stranded here

with sand and salt and the slant of a certain sun.
The cave on the beach is empty, a solitude except
for the modest cloaked in shadow. Pretend the cave
is a house and you're home at an oval table set

with pewter. Goose is served. An imaginary friend
resurfaces: sunrise followed later, in marked-off hours,
by sunset. Waves rise and collapse, collapse and
withdraw, withdraw, regroup. To name this "barren"

rather than an example of a style known for its lack-
luster is to miss the point completely. It is crucial
that we notice subtleties of raven against sable, love
against eagerness, hear murmurs and distinguish

whether they are whisperings or heavy palm leaves.
It takes commitment. The moon has begun to falter;
the sea hovers over a body holding its breath, waiting
for predators, a cloud. This is as good a start as any.

## For My Sister

I awake dangerously low in resources, also
it is early, later than this. Dogmatically six times

throughout night. Physical comfort is more
important than what I have to say of previous

generations, how they conducted themselves
during the war years or how I met you accidentally,

how each of us did. Held hands and walked over
bridges before the novels were written about night

mist shredding into morning grass, the state and its
modifications. At sea admirals were at rest.

Now it is six past five, five past six, tints zigzag
the parlor floor. Each distinct light has a name

once valued sufficiently to discern, as with other
natural phenomena. We should rejoice there are

no more plagues, just intervals of misfortune
followed by longer intervals also named misfortune

or referred to as approximately forever and
getting worse. Twisted in thin sheets, remain heroic,

uncomfortably explaining your wrists are uncut.
An outstretched hand is nothing much to write

a letter home about or the sun lowering behind
the maples or any other tree whose leaves might

fade scarlet. Nothing must break to have value—
weather, tiny bones, teacups—in order to confirm

what transported you here, captive to earth,
with watchful guardianship, even jealousy.

# Some Statements Have Been Made

A generation is on the rise in two
metropolitan cities. One to the east,
the other to the west. On the west
coast mud slips from a hill and a mountain
is made of it. On the east coast the trains
have stopped and a generation is whining;
their feet tired, no one is making
what he or she deserves. It will take time,
a fashion season at best, or from the
broadcast of this weekend's award show
to the announcement of next year's
nominees. Enjoy yourselves, there is no
such thing as negative attention. If the
spotlight falls on your generation, or
even if it doesn't, you perform. It's called
work ethic. My generation is a good person
making poor choices; we are absent from
the rally, the march, the sit-in, since
the form of our content does not require
collective action. Your generation is drafting
a manifesto. It is cold on the street—
our government acknowledges this, as do
our bodies, my generation's and yours.
All people are equal. The local park is
covered in snow, it is noted for its beauty,
its *transcendent goodness*, its tendency
to disrupt. Both my generation and yours
take notice. My generation quotes
the Turkish proverb "Before you love,
learn to run through the snow leaving
no footprint." Birds from around the country
descend on the park, soon there will be

increased knowledge of their intelligence.
Your generation wrote: All actions have
consequences, and it is the character of
an individual that determines actions.
My generation stood all night in snow
to speak with your generation, and your
generation spoke: When the great egret
stands in the snow, it is no longer white.
Your generation pointed to the mountains
and said: Which one is without significance?
Listen to this, the snow falls honestly.

## Love, the Proven Deterrent

Today, in stillness, the weather
  is crazy circling; an injured

bedbug, its horizon leg broken.
  In the dining room, another halo

slipping into noose, you sprinkled
  sawdust into my eyes. It absorbs

the wetness tracked in. It depends
  how one looks at it: Askew, acutely

with a rigid neck from stargazing.
  It was last evening. Or the last

minus one, when the oceanic
  feeling was an exquisite lion

or a revolving globe. The resting
  worlds opposed disintegration.

No one sang, *Dust to dust we all fall.*
  Everything was rosy: A figure

held a woman's head reduced to
  curves and blue light, late evening

and the opportunity for the moon
  already empty or emptying.

# A Tendency toward Mysticism

All I wanted was to take you somewhere,
to be lonely. I could never stand it.

Somewhere out of here. That was forever
ago or yesterday; wherever the voice

stretches from mist, from an idea,
it ends with the moon swallowing trees

and depositing them on houses, trains,
gazebos, a pond of thin ice. I couldn't

understand, had other worries, wasn't
interested in folklore or self-mythologizing.

I didn't think anything. I pulled myself
together like a man once on a cliff,

then walking away. I could feel my stomach,
was always glad it was over. There will be

a last conversation in order to get
close enough to touch you. We will

shed under separate skins. I can do this.
Say the things you say. Say hello. *Hello.*

I can do this. There is a growing
apprehension that my peers are listening.

I enjoyed our silence, was suited for it.
I am not cynical. I am a man with two

feet on the ground. I drink coffee, smoke,
am not a coward. I can only report

what I know, like that man standing
on a cliff. This is a sophisticated thought.

The human body wants desperately to die
and does. I had said what I never meant.

## *from* A Thorn of Sonnets

A mirror leaning reflecting setting
and nausea—the drift toward pretending
to exist is encouraged by time, by faculties
that direct desires and the senses guided
by the repetition of shame. After night
comes day. It requires a remedy unlikely
to bear false witness. This sense of the world
as a psychic storm transforms general life
into a state of concealment, a brook flanked
by a willow, locks of hair, and pearls
carrying reverberations. More generally,
it was a philosophical joke depending
on the distinction between inner reality
and outward appearance.

# Poem

A jar does not sing its contents,
it either savors or forgets. If one
fact has lost a particle, the jar
that holds your thought begins
to quiver with such misfortune.
There's no good degree of opinion
to back us up. The jar left out
on a dock in all species of weather,
like a body, takes its fill and empties
what it cannot hold. I looked out:
The ocean was catastrophic. Moon-
beams were serene, each a shroud,
fell as we were taught, not from
a heavenly body but a construction
of dust. We no longer wait for
the world to change. I place a jar
out to catch the rain, to start over
again. A jar once polished is not
a cause but a vessel waiting for stems,
for stones. No matter the cause,
you place a jar on the table. Let's
place a jar on an ark and shove it
to sea. Let the sea be catastrophic,
let the jar glimpse the natives,
the savages, the civilized, but let it
wash ashore, find itself far gone.

# Work Product

I am here breathing
heavy into one end
of the receiver

in order to reassure you
I am here
on one end breathing.

I find it is important
a stranger feels
as though he or she

has just entered
a clearing where
a majestic bear, rare

so late in the season,
nears a pond. I practice
breathing at home

into an embroidered pillow
shaped like a parrot.
In the morning

I take my body
to where it belongs.
It is exhausting belonging

to anything at all.
In the morning
a small head

attaches itself
to my body.
I must concentrate

on the job at hand.
The phone is ringing
and I think

you were asking
and I don't
believe I have the answer.

I admit I was practicing
breathing. I was off
somewhere else thinking

of the whales
that have beached themselves.
Yes,

I was somewhere thinking
of the crowd
watching the whales.

The phone is ringing
and LINE ONE is a story
of talent and genius.

LINE TWO, it is your mother
and you are crying again.
Don't cry. I am touching

your shoulder.

# A Fifth Memory

Let's not speak of ravens, keyholes at twilight, subjects
immediate to observation appearing partly as a doctrine
of chance. It is unlike me to dispute what is grand.

A cloud field can herald distress, command numbers
to fragment, but the rainfall lacked compulsion: how
birds listed as unclean were birds of prey, not a model

for conduct. Every day began with trust; segments
fitted together like small bodies of animals and plants.
Arriving home, a touch positioned your face upright

regardless of industrious wind. Restore me to that
then, however streaked with gloom, however riddled
through with worm and sorrow. Part of the problem

was mandatory participation, the other your radiant
neck from certain sadness, half-feelings in August
or the will to walk many-sided. Restore me to a prior

arena beyond where this letter fills a hand mildly. There
exists no such thing as three beginnings. Earlier gestures
were vague in declaring intention, and what the echo

from the cliff responds with is a general void, minor
modifications in mood like English weather. Restore
the song to its bird, bird its egg, egg its concept. This world

mirrored a wonder formerly praised until we discovered
the structure of horror in all inventions. I anticipated
otherwise, the arrangement of light on a woodland stream

to dazzle, a red fox paused on a hilltop to restore
a condition decayed. What could determine the next
question? What answer could halt the mind and its written

description from an eternity grazing on itself? What answer
could relinquish such control or once more bury it?

# Vows

We are gathered here today
separately together. Each of you

removed with caution from
a previous life to this ceremonial

clearing acknowledged as this.
We welcome loved ones and lingering

spheres witnessed at night. You have
each forgotten encounters and are mature

for having these lives. Could you have
lived them better without the other?

We are here to watch anonymous weather
on this day, before family and friends,

divided between one hand you hold,
the other empty as long as you can live.

# Prologue and Epilogue

As a result of youth I was given intention
  at an address. Adult voices splintered
like patterns from leaves wallpapering
  shapes above my bed, their exact
purpose unknown. I went elsewhere,
  burned sandalwood, placed an apple
washed in the blue clouds of the blue god
  Krishna; sat in a dark condominium
cross-legged and chanting, anticipating
  voltage to spherically exit my fingers.
My wishes couldn't be harnessed.
  Right hand dirty it took more to disorder.
It's necessary I blame disease, echoes
  intertwined with local authority dead-
ending me until misplaced and waking
  in stranger basements. Placed anything
in my mouth to placebo through frequent
  nights. Each episode reforming another.
Don't misunderstand: I agree every person
  is granted the right to make peace,
let compassion unfurl publicly at a podium
  or alone in woodlands forever spoken
of in the future tense as a master bedroom
  or cul-de-sac. One performs as one must,
the voices disintegrate across history,
  and I'm learning to take it presently.
In this room, I swallow the same blueness
  each day with a glass of filtered water.
Take it when you remember, right upon
  thinking. Time filters, cells divide, disappear
into a summer, or wherever I affix myself I settle.
  In a crosstown cab, on couches, the park,

together privately talking about shared
experience to establish a definition:
The machinery in you malfunctions in me.
I'm taking it personally. This is what is left—
little difference. I have recollections I would have
liked to relate to you. This is what is left,
a small container with ash and rabbit-sized bones.
Wet earth, dry earth, it's a hole.

## *from* A Thorn of Sonnets

An alliance struck, needing reassurance,
this rain shows regular order across lakes,
the ends of earth where we continue
to distinguish and then, distinguishing,
rest on the wooden floor, shutting eyes
for extensive naps. Anxieties are resolved
in the brightness of dark more often than
not before morning light shades the room
like a recent event, wishing to sleep it off.
One good turn deserves this other, and,
if deserving, the mouth will open, a hand
will find a place on the body to garnish
like mythical animals woven into a tapestry,
red and gold, a dark room conserves.

# Tending to Degrade

It is conceivable pain will affix, building from present
states of previous illnesses and uncured by changes
in air. It is conceivable in the absence of explanations
the air within is circulated in a variety of shapes
imagined here, as I have been coached, in a soothing
hue. Difficulties arise if one imposes upon them.

Take off my coat. Separate what I think from what is
actually going down, one's balance being dependent
on distance understood as finite to the unaided eye.
I'm uncertain that's factual. Take a seat and with this
pencil satisfy the questions regarding graveyard
grass and how often thoughts reside there: once.

More than once a week. It is conceivable an odd
premonition could mimic a real one, and spontaneously
casual symptoms unchecked and subject to perils,
all manner of varied stimuli and shocks, will advance.
Such data, when reproduced in an interior voice
actively devoid of anxiety as I have been coached,

resigns to common sense, management of time, and
schedules. Dim the lights. Breakthroughs do happen,
though require a village or a rough draft of a village,
an army of horsemen, rowers, or footmen over
indeterminate topography. Granted, it is conceivable
to find comfort in the soul as an ancient constellation

derived from a reptilian god and subject to storm winds
or, if such assurances are unnatural to your constitution,
settle for staring out an oval window at the sea with designs
to prevent further morbid conditions. Dim the lights.
Little is available to aid the passage of night, yet it is incumbent
to try. Scientifically, there's always a chance the sky will

unhinge, but in the final analysis rational arrangements
must be made. It is conceivable we're beating a dead horse,
even regions of calm, interior or subject to catalogs of weather,
prolong a journey. It is conceivable this is how it starts, here
out this window, white birds, white birds, gray water, the name
of the shapes, as of now, harboring no intent to harm.

# Poem to Help Me Help You

When asleep I trusted you
not to run off with the first

ecologist; to relinquish doubt
and watch over me languishing

like a mediocre gimp when
your prints are what actively

marked my broken instruments,
detecting halftones between

land and ocean. Rust patches
spread and actions conducted

are relieved in a sense with a nostalgic
piece of lint placed in a bell jar

and titled *Snowstorm from Our*
*Window on Union Street.* Unable

to return home, sadness can
be transformed into self-interest

others admire while away from me
on this side of the mountain.

I didn't feel the seismic activity
sometimes shaking, aloof to

consent and displacing ground.
When asleep, waves move through

the earth's crust. Let's not make
any more of it, the dangerous

applications to a private life,
the various stakeholders affected.

Take it easy, even the scientific
method is subjective and

temporary. Apparently, we are
born this way, operating at a loss

over the course of a night, over
the course of a single sleep;

a procedure replays corridor
gossip, household knowledge

and signals are interrupted,
and we wake with a zeal to study

honeybees and the altering climate.
Henceforth I blame you for the

ka-bang, the new restlessness,
the rush for gold in due course

degraded in form. Let's not make
much more of lost time

compressed. It is impossible
to record. As to the measure

of martyrdom or myth, a hunger
whorishly uncontrolled defeats

itself into loving like a whore.
I'm not supposed to talk. But

I could have, should have, and will.

# Evidence of Absence

Forensically speaking, sun and day, moon and month,
are all the same word. A mirror held before a face
having just exhaled smoke, on a day without prescriptions,
frames the failure the mind is entangled with; it need not,
of course, be attached to any specific person, though,
speaking now with the requisite clinical experience
to form an objective opinion with a reasonable degree
of certainty, it is. I'm speaking of qualities themselves
and not the names by which they are known. Life bears
such scrutiny. Under any formal system, be it logic
or penmanship, there is an infinite amount of downward
slant. Regardless, we must conclude something, call it
what you may, consensus, conspiracy, or oral contract;
one is bound to acknowledge the rain, practical matters
of dressing, answers to riddles: What is at the beginning
of every end and at the end of every place? I'm speaking now
more of the silence which, by simply speaking, we break,
and I have sworn an oath, a service to acknowledge
relevant events as such might have taken place. Stretches
of time, longer than hours, let me rephrase this: By some
calculation, phases of moon, or mechanical device, and early,
punctual, or late, time passes. Neither you nor I can judge.
Or let me rephrase that: I want to leave here a better person.
The other option to return to our regularly scheduled
programming, place sneakered feet on the coffee table,
ceiling fan circulating ash clouds with a hint of mint. And I won't

pass judgment. Neither will I condone "cries for help" absent a genuine attempt to die. On inspecting further, facial muscles, habit of eye conduct, all range of nonverbal instances reflected and predicting how these simple acts would feel in different settings: a grand hotel, on a sailboat—or wherever else my active fantasy places you. Proceeding thus I traveled the limits of failure, the form of our partnership, noting people gain liabilities, however total a state of entertainment they keep. This may be simple enough. It seems to me there can be but one answer. On inspecting, there were other options. No one judge passes a decisive verdict.

# Kingdom for a Horse

Years without thought
went time until wind

stilled. A world is heaven
until it inherits a name.

A creature cannot appear
from the house of light

on the hill. Years grow
into a ring or vice versa;

henceforth a consecutive
thought begins in a valley,

thinking deer for antelope,
magistrate for doctor,

containment for commitment.
Garlands for your neck, ghosts

to haunt. The snake charmers
lay their charges to rest.

Wind places the heart first
in the sea and then in fables.

# III

# Institutional Memory

It took forever to arrive at a conclusion
though it hovered before us, where you
placed your eyes it wasn't. It goes without
saying the moon is full with minor noises
and will break gently as night breaks as
a wave of thought over the idea of your body
in my bed. Damaged goods are damaged,
and this day, a year from last night today,
echoes in a square. The morning might
remove fog, replace it with blue flowers
with names from literature, bring news
of new disease or your eventual pain beneath
the dogwood days from bloom. Gradually
our faces feel a future, our gaze provides
a room, a door figuratively leading,
your figure faithfully exact, exactly leaning.
We knew it was there, making truth less true,
compelling vision from flaws amplifying
lovemaking in the dark, didactic breath near
my neck. Knowledge obstructs sunlight filtering
in, and I continue sleeping with a triangle
of thought, resenting air yet continuing to
breathe, which is akin to caring. It happened
so immediately, it happened yesterday,
is happening again. You should have ended
like this room locked in my throat.

## To the Modest, but Real

Historically, development is
a measure of knowledge.

Questions are asked and
unanswered in a two-value

system, and it happens
names become clouds

searching for shape. Hover
between bone and skin.

Often a number of factors
contribute to conflict.

Grass bends beneath a boy;
earth cannot alter with every

pinpointing sensation, and near
sunset he refuses to accept

a dual world. He asks himself,
What are the relative merits

of these positions? He considers
the same lines: Black are the horses

of the black moon. A refrain
of a refrain. This is only

one example of dignity.
And it happens one word

is used for another like the half-
dead carrying on among us.

# Temple Dream

I find myself here, again after hours,
  a blue room in Belgium, velvet ropes
released—the kneeling man amongst
  those that stand watch over me
as if I were appointed through ritual
  bloodletting or a proxy passing
a pewter goblet back and forth
  at intervals of seven. I'm unable
to convey to any willing listeners
  the several mysteries, phases, or
personal suffering felt differently
  in my various muscles that placed
me here. I don't mean to suggest
  I'm withholding, only that, simply,
I was born with a mysterious gift.
  For example, when alone in my office
I imagine the phone ringing and it rings
  with the voice of the body pictured
on the screen of my eyes. I was chosen,
  set aside early when my top teeth
grew before those below, identifying
  me to the elders as a candidate
for additional research. On later
  occasions birds approached as I sat
on city benches. I don't mean to imply
  there are insights I could articulate
and you would fail to adequately grasp.
  What I want to say is you will learn more
witnessing than listening, as if caught
  in a dream in which, depending on
the specific nature of your ailment, you are
  either the animal hot on the scent or

the animal breathing quietly beneath
  the earth. What I mean to say is, God
created for every disease a remedy,
  there is nothing death can't efface,
nothing that moans and doesn't recline.
  My face clouds over and fails to report
any clouding, any local criminal mischief.
  I have taken an oath that I will hide
here until I run out of breath.

# No Matter the Details

Inside this gray building, the aftereffects of hours
illuminate a sickly demeanor cultivated in shade
as the sun pauses behind a chance form as I am
turning on a swivel chair. Inside or out, we are kept
under the sky like a prototype for places departed

or inextricable from. The symbolism is personal
inside this architecture, all symbols are. Always the same
disturbance grows bodies, surrounds us, me. I leave
my door open. Set bias aside, turning down a familiar
corridor, beige carpet runner well-worn with a given

course inside a building between floors. It is natural,
when surrounded by figures in a mood one wishes
a curse upon to conjure an errand to walk away.
Another package has arrived in the lobby. I'm closing
the door behind me. Whatever the cause, defer

further implications until a coffee break, a silent moment
in a commercial space beside the atrium's abstract sculpture
titled for a general or statesman. Invariably whatever
the design, inventions hold us in their gaze. You can't
forget where you're from. I try to forget I'm barely here

myself, half-awake to having given up, stationed like
a head with good ear placed firmly on pillow, the other
attending a vibrating almost overheard, indications
merely of conversations going on. I will smoke less,
control my temper, smile at the customers. In hindsight

it's a practical matter: Conversations originate in errors,
most commonly theirs, and left unresolved develop
into a portable darkness carried in facial structures.
No matter the factors, the details recall the repetitive stress
in recalling anything at all. It is natural to remember

the increased cost of cigarettes. It will pass, five minutes
becomes ten—I wait the length of a summer's storm
with analogous feeling. It's possible if a feeling appears
just once in a certain light, inside a gray building, we are
justified in holding that in similar conditions it reappears

always the same. It's possible in hindsight it has to end.
This day, all feeling, with my head on a pillow adopting
the course of the moon: mostly present most of the time,
distributing seven versions of night with six thousand
visible stars and fifty-two cloud types passing like facsimiles.

## Our Bodies Will Relearn to Float

Dove gray lit from within

Azure with a chance of rain

So many roses performing

The exact same schedule

# A Finely Worked Coffin

Each rap at your hatch with bronze
knocker shaped like vulture goes
unanswered. To be such a figure
of distinction is no simple destination.
Be still and do not splinter.
Each elaborate lotus was painted
for scenery, to play dull and
listen to you. Be still. No power
of will can crack a lock.

That is your pleasure, forever
at rest in the hiding place of night,
no hawk waiting. The candlelight
from the altar is unable to determine
your body. Rest assured. You are safe
inside with eyes shut and what looks
dead is. Certainly my faith will
not do; you are not the figure
your shape suggests though you
recall a figure that walked in
the walking light of a midafternoon
in the year of our Lord.

Be still, there is value in what
does not shatter. Your eyes, once
pearls, robbed and replaced with coral.
Harbored within this structure you are
safe; the new dawn spoken of in scriptures,
in speech acts, is not yet possible.

## *from* A Thorn of Sonnets

On this day of rest we require an emblem
proving the harps and small bells determined
to be released from the phonograph are
transcendental. Each note carries a digression
but God hates imagination more than progress
and identifies seven ways to hang from
the neck. Empires fall, this one, that one.
The heart aches old with earth, dirty, misused
with inventions to modify a flower.
Ultimately what is developed is inseparable
from the original source of pleasure which
we may now call *magnetism.* The characteristics
echo and echo an affirmation, until we forget
the ceremonies composed to keep us earthbound.

# A Clock between Hours

Frost covers further ground
than anticipated. Covers

two resting bodies. A field
or a large part of field is flickering,

producing more noise than the light
it reflects. Under the frost, acoustics

are engineered; with a mouth near
an ear, speech is distinguished

from touching. Gently these bodies
create a pulse when knocked together.

The pulse is flickering. Forgive that
which flickers involuntarily

as water, as a heart from reflex
produces more noise than light.

A light will eventually descend.
Forgive that which is sleeping,

such as plant, stone. Forgive
our bodies which are not one organism.

## Home Invasion

From the month of data
  I retrieve myself.
Night rusts. It goes
  without saying
shadows are containers,
  I'm saying it: There is
no safe angle of approach.
  Black cat, black cat,
hours ago my friend,
  accompanied by other
thoughts, derived
  from an original now
retarded, a root grown
  around a shovel un-
powered by imagination.
  I know you, origin
beyond mine called
  something unnamed.
I can see you anywhere,
  particularly corners,
curtains, misplaced
  door, hinge pulled apart.

# After Reading This Poem

After reading this poem I think of other poems,
bath salts, parking fees, over-the-counter cold
medicine, child care, misc., fitness, and dental.
After reading this poem I ask if anyone has read
anything good lately. I would be interested
in hearing from someone who has. After reading
this I want to know your opinion on white people
writing poems about Indians, the aesthetic
terms *beauty* and *balance*, or the terms *sin* and
*grace*, which all reflect something in the mind,
even if they can't be defined objectively.
We should at least comment on this. Lately
though, I have been interested in the disinterested
reader. Or the certain gist of the thing that kept
reminding me of that drawing of what looks like
a duck from one angle looks like a rabbit
from another. After reading this poem the class
was asked on a scale from 1 (almost never)
to 5 (almost always) how often they use attributes
including: how the poem fits the model in the photo;
style; care instructions; and color—in determining
what poems to buy. The catalog defines a poem
as a monopoly of power. In this poem the same
moon noticing a deserted world, emptied of life
and meaning, appears once as the moon, once
as an infectious airborne disease, and once more,
because these things happen in threes, as a collection
of Dutch still lifes searchable online. Ultimately
this poem is about emotional recovery, which is
a type of economic indicator for eventual behavior,
for only pleasure has value, though a third of
the class feels the sale of this poem to "tween"

females is corrupt. A third thinks a poem shouldn't
be a friend with benefits. The other third
believes the pleasures of this poem are in
the way it enables the development of the poet
to be traced from divorced parents, to Krishna,
to pharmaceuticals, to recovery, and in this regard
is a type of 21st century afternoon special.

# A Man of Distinction

He was filled with hat honor and refused to remove
his tricorne indoors. Technicality was built on technicality,

so said the whispering campaign. The whole border
might burn for it. He preached the dogma of the absence

of dogma. Much of the appeal turned out to be plain
old escapism and the shade of trees, local trees.

Not to mention the geography had its way with the people,
the people their way with the whipping post, the post

with the rack, and the rack with the gallows, who in turn
had their way with the internal pulpit of fire and hammer.

He had wished to become an apostle of elbow room,
but it lacked explicit theological defense. He believed

in the Beloved, the good mind, the waking promise, in inner
glory rather than the outer husk. What he hated was

only a mirror. To learn and to act became one, no matter
the dividing line and its history—all history is malleable,

even his. Believe it or not, there were no structures
yet, except for one in blueprints carried over on ship:

a church tower containing a much-loved bell cast back
in the Middle Ages. The distinction he drew between weapon

and tool was the first to lose meaning. The bell above
rang a unifying principle until it shattered into spoons.

# Poem Unfinished

A partial moon hangs from a tree
clarifying the vacant coast; dreamers

in stages are lured by forgetfulness.
On the surface talk devastates

remembering: What is viewed holds
an example of speech, something circles

and closes and closes until one position
over another is known. A decade discussed

over the span of a decade, eventually
paraphrased in a catalog of dates, pictures

of snowfall, a bouquet of miniature lilacs
photographed, framed, and placed above

a hand-carved armoire located in a secret
room painted antique white. The reflection

in the veneer shivers. Where is it stated
*yellow* is the color of disease? The century

continues to defragment at irregular
intervals, the hillside, the error. You start

with nowhere, you start from blood.
Lord, you give dominion rose-colored

and almost-dead. The hills are 25%
complete; the sky has yet to materialize.

## *from* A Thorn of Sonnets

The frost last year broke the crystal
air we might associate with a pure
spring morning near an old temple
beside a clear lake where the moon
grew full and floated away through
a mist emphasizing the glow
from the elm beside the gate where
I traveled last spring to the house
of definitive flowers which is endless
like a holy light cast from a lantern
set for a coming friend or yellow
finches flashing in an imperial grove
where homing birds sleep with lights
extinguished in their heads.

## What Prevails

After much thoroughness, what prevails
is exhaustion, glowing fluorescent lights.
I sleep it off as both guilty and innocent must.

I am only one at a time, move from the one
to the next; no spectrum of ideas shines
from above. Sunlight appears as cloth

covering the path. It does not lead to a pile
of ashes, to branches like words you cannot
reach. The arms you grow will reach, bend

the branches back toward thought.

## Severance

I have come to the desired point, the evening of the 16th
mostly clear from nine until midnight, attention
was directed almost entirely to the northwest though
I turned my eye, a few times, to the east. I made
no committed reports. Quite possibly I overlooked

circumstances with opportunity to explain, misunderstood
facts containing certain sinister details, both social
and psychological, positions undermined in advance
prior to the greenness of moss. It is well known
I made no such reports, no descriptions in person

or via mobile phone, but this is supplemented by
the general communication of others, what they have
been told, in confidence or otherwise, or have
observed in interactions or lack thereof. I do find
it incumbent on me, given this platform, to reiterate

I offer no excuses, don't point to a childhood spent
caring for pets, adolescent years of skeptical reserve.
I made no public statement to my countrymen and now
is not the moment to look back over a thousand foreign
grasses, waiting for redemption to take shape. I admit

I waited with an expectation of locating you across the river
more ancient than funeral structures. Lonely territory;
the night of the 16th, my journal notes, music left car radios
somewhere. It was a mistake inferring the world was
an island rather than an interlude advancing. I stood,

each stillness disrupting another, looked for signs in a field
guide and cemeteries, thought you would return the way
rain falls like previous rain or silent mountains continue
inventing new snows. It should be known I suffered, slept
one eye up, over and over the same anxieties until a piece

of quiet. An exhausted bird, storm-tossed, arrived, drawing
slowly familiar like detailed statements. It was naïve
to subscribe to a belief in auguries, to empower such creatures
with speech, and furthermore to listen: The degree to which
one is ground to pieces fails to alleviate the burden.

No one remembers I was sick while the sun bent from where
to where, waiting, each stillness another until I believed
I had come to identify numerous apparitions, if not black
in art, mysterious in thought, and I followed myself away
from myself. I know actions committed, and here I mean

imagined, without concern for faith, have left me half-
demolished. It should be noted my expressed wish that
they be buried like a premonition dreamed by an Emperor
before the advent of papyrus—but it stays with a person—
repairs an invisible thread around a nameless finger.

# Poem

Contrary to fanciful allegations, this poem
is not a vestige of a pagan temple. No
such temple ever existed in this book.

Though the curve of a moonlit coast
banging against a moonlit rock resembles
the curve of a church bell made by Belgian

monks in the Middle Ages. That much this
poem contains, as does another poem about
early America. Everything else changes,

based on what we know thus far. In this poem
strange noises upstairs mean children are
communing with the dead. No light shines

from underneath the door. It is a mouth,
shown convulsively, that tells me what
the dead are rapping on the window about.

Take a look at a mustard seed or at a point
on the end of a pencil. Imagine what a mountain
looks like. It's huge! In this poem

God insists we stamp out reality before reality
stamps us, that history provides defining
moments from which we judge where we are

against where we have been. On the mountain
a mirror is set up to frame the view behind us.
It is almost real enough to touch, which is how

this poem remembers our time together.

# The Gentle Sleep

Empty I slept, remembering how others
feared sleep, feared the likeness between

a fading consciousness and permanent
escape drifting out past smoke, past particles

of last-call conversations. It's uneasy,
this waking life, but drugs work quickly,

not quickly enough. Empty I slept through
foghorns, birth names, and the Midwest,

through a darkness that favors a future
with a limited preview, an alias for everything

in every form, position, and time, and then
its reproduction. We should agree this

wakefulness is an irritation and thus I slept,
remembering myself as odds and ends,

as the general sadness of German folk ballads—
slept regardless of meals late in the day, of undue

quantities of tea, or of the mental activity connected
to business or debts. Empty I slept through

the state funeral and the various rites of passage
with a customary fear of all imaginary things.

# The Late Interior

After humans were placed in the sky
and returned from the sky ambiguously
different, after clouds launched across

the range of reference or icicles melted
in Rhode Island, after the sun lowered
over hills like propaganda pamphlets

dropped and found half a century later
for sale on the internet as a melancholy
keepsake to hang adjacent the pantry,

grass grows beneath my feet and I try
to remember where I am, after observations
note a number of repulsive particles

held solidly together as a force cradling
me here, undeserving of serious attention.
After smoke exits this wood-grain pipe,

after sensing a resemblance in the hand
holding the pipe, the smoke finds refuge
in a cardigan, the teapot, ceramics, cups

always close at hand, as is silence, shifting
satellite to satellite, one municipality
to the next. After threats of rain the rain

moved off the coast, the same subject
is continued at 72 degrees, breezy, little
or no content, none, and so in a moment

of bewilderment one phones the help desk
and is placed on hold, a piano composition
slowly patterns thought. After the same

subject is exhausted, as in many cases,
by laziness, non-inquiry, false shame, or
fear of man and worldly motives, I will finish

at my own pace before the figures appear
with torches or flashlights or else ringing
the doorbell. After the last firm handshake,

data clouds, table talk, and today's exaltation
at the red door on a secluded street,
after despair, industrial affairs, sloppy

monopolies, bounties, and prohibitions
against which the worthlessness or worth
of everything must be weighed alone,

after the patient efforts to rouse oneself
to seek fair treatment, to travel from home,
I travel from home, I seek fair treatment.

## Acknowledgments

The epigraph is taken from *The Sorrows of Young Werther*, translated by Michael Hulse.

I'd like to thank the editors and staff of the following journals in which some of these poems first appeared: *811 Books*, *American Poetry Review*, *The Awl*, *Bomb*, *Boston Review*, *Columbia: A Journal of Literature and Art*, *Denver Quarterly*, *Electronic Poetry Review*, *Fence*, *Iowa Review*, *jubilat*, *La Petite Zine*, *Lit*, *The Literary Review*, *Maggy*, *Modern Review*, *OmniVerse*, *Pleiades*, *RealPoetik*, *Similar Peaks*, and *Tin House*.

"A Tendency Toward Mysticism" was reprinted in *Satellite Convulsions* (Tin House Books, 2008).

"The Gentle Sleep" also appeared as a broadside by All Along Press for the Fort Gondo Poetry Series.

"Majestic Interlude," "Community of Inquiry," "A Home for Head Injuries," and "For Example" appeared on the PEN American Center website.

* * *

The deepest heartfelt thanks goes to friends and teachers for their support and encouragement with these poems, most especially, Joshua Beckman, Robert Casper, Seth Fleischman, Graham Foust, Matthea Harvey, Brenda Hillman, Brigid Hughes, Andrew Kenower, Naomi Leibowitz, Lynn Melnick, Charlie Never, Alice Quinn, Matthew Rohrer, and Matthew Zapruder. And to the first readers of many of these poems: Stefania Heim and Jennifer Kronovet, and from first draft to last—Timothy Donnelly. And of course my family, Anne Fletcher and Alfred Lauer, and my new family, Gretchen Scott.

Special thanks to Ryan Murphy and Martha Rhodes.

Brett Fletcher Lauer is the deputy director of the Poetry Society of America and the poetry editor at *A Public Space*. He is the co-editor of *Isn't It Romantic: 100 Love Poems by Younger American Poets* (Wave, 2004) and his poems have appeared in *American Poetry Review*, *Boston Review*, *Fence*, *Harper's*, *Tin House*, and elsewhere.